# Intermediate Racquetball Drills

Intermediate Racquetball Drills

Jean Sauser and Arthur Shay

Contemporary Books, Inc.
Chicago

Library of Congress Cataloging in Publication Data

Sauser, Jean.
   Intermediate racquetball drills.

   1. Racquetball.   I. Shay, Arthur.   II. Title.
GV1017.R3S284   1981   796.34'3   80-70644
ISBN 0-8092-5926-5 (pbk.)   AACR2

Copyright © 1981 by Jean Sauser and Arthur Shay
All rights reserved
Published by Contemporary Books, Inc.
180 North Michigan Avenue, Chicago, Illinois 60601
Manufactured in the United States of America
Library of Congress Catalog Card Number: 80-70644
International Standard Book Number: 0-8092-5926-5

Published simultaneously in Canada by
Beaverbooks, Ltd.
150 Lesmill Road
Don Mills, Ontario M3B 2T5
Canada

Contents

Introduction   vii

1. The Challenge   1

2. Warming Up   4

3. Drills for Intermediate Players   6
    Off-the-front-wall drill   *6*
    Straight kill drop and hit drill for forehand and backhand   *9*
    Corner pinch drop and hit drill   *13*
    Side wall drill   *14*
    Corner drill—bounce in   *19*
    Ceiling ball drill   *23*
    Shooting ceiling ball off back wall drill   *27*

4. Two-Player Drills   31
    Running back for deep court shot drill   *31*
    Pinch drill   *36*
    Fly-kill drill   *40*
    Running to front court to cover a corner drill   *42*
    Ceiling ball and shot drill   *45*
    Drive serve and service return drill   *50*

Introduction

Covering the racquetball pros as official photographer for *National Racquetball* magazine and the U.S. Racquetball Association, I have worked with every one of the racquetball pros, including Marty Hogan, Charlie Brumfield, Steve Keeley, Steve Strandemo, Dave Peck, Jennifer Harding, Shannon Wright, Heather McKay, Peggy Steding, and Jean Sauser, my coauthor.

The question the pros have asked me most frequently is, "Why do you have to take so many shots with that motorized camera to get a few good ones?" I generally reply, "Why do you have to practice the same boring shot two or three hundred times each time you practice?"

"Boring? Why there's nothing more exciting than doing a shot three hundred times—say for a morning workout on changing my forehand slightly," Charlie Brumfield once told me. "When I practice ceiling shots I may do two hundred, just trying to hit a three-inch circle on the ceiling every time." (For those few intermediate racquetballers who don't know, Brumfield is racquetball's Babe Ruth.)

viii Introduction

As all of our best teachers put it, in one way or another: practice makes perfect.

Certainly, for intermediate players who want to progress one step beyond their everyday opponents or the gang they meet at regional tournaments, practice is the only answer. But what kind of practice?

Working as teacher-coach for intermediate and advanced players of both sexes, Jean Sauser has developed a series of simple intermediate-player drills that are custom-designed to add points to your game and, if you're aging somewhat, save you lots of steps. The stamina you save will be your own!

Diligence is necessary to achieving racquetball goals, and these drills are for serious players who know what pinch shots and cross-court passes are, and who look forward to tournament play as a learning experience.

The drills are somewhat elastic, allowing for variation and creativity. If there's an area in which you need work, don't hesitate to program a practice drill around it, in keeping with the tough pace of this book. After doing these drills for two weeks, I found myself photographing pro Steve Keeley for *Sports Illustrated.* Giving away twenty pounds and twenty-five years, I was nevertheless able to defeat Keeley two games to one. Of course, he was sick and tired at the time—but these drills *work.* Said Keeley, "It *had* to be those drills. Just look at the old guy. He's a fireplug."

Arthur Shay

1
The Challenge

Both the player who is progressing rapidly and the player who has arrived at competency or even great skill encounter a common problem: it becomes increasingly difficult to find a challenging, adequate opponent. Many times these players are better off practicing by themselves than playing people they can beat easily. This book is designed in part for the loners or near loners who wish to practice intermediate play creatively. *Intermediate Racquetball Drills* is also intended for tournament players who arrive a day or a few hours before a match; they can devote their spare time to these drills and shore up weak spots in offense or defense.

Not every intermediate player is an up-and-coming Marty Hogan who can derive a good practice round from a B player opponent. These drills are designed to help an intermediate player work out with an equally good player or a less skilled player to the benefit of both.

Ambitious players who do not have coaching available, or

who can't afford it, can use these drills the way some weight trainers use their muscles—one against the other in moves designed to build, build, build. The ingrained American do-it-yourself spirit is alive and well in racquetball. These drills should find favor with players determined to win and persevere on their own. The drills in this book are also designed to get the intermediate player thinking about shot selection once shot execution has become second nature. Making good, instinctive choices instantly is the secret of most superb athletic performance. When that ball comes at you, the better player you are, the more alternative shots are available for you to make. Killing the ball means never having to think, "I'm sorry."

Concentration—focusing on the thing you are doing at the moment—is the secret weapon of almost all successful athletes. Shutting out the entire world except the job of getting that racquet to that ball, or that body to that ball, is an instinct or a developed skill of the very greatest. Bjorn Borg has it. Marty Hogan has it. The great baseball batters have it. Former handball champion Paul Haber once said, "I even look at the ball during time-outs."

You should focus on the ball in doing these drills. Think about the skills you are developing and practicing. If you are working on a mental grocery list and hitting the ball at the same time, you might as well go shopping and forget practicing. Training your mind not to wander is not easy, but it can be done—and racquetball is the darling of many businesspeople who feel that the sport *forces* the player to concentrate on the ball. This, of course, prevents the mind from dwelling on business problems, adding to racquetball's value as an all-around physical and mental activity.

So concentrate on the ball, think about your form, and imagine your opponent in the proper spot for your exercise to be most beneficial.

The final ingredient is repetition. You should practice a drill only as long as you can legitimately concentrate on it. For some players that can be an hour, for others only fifteen minutes. A half hour to an hour is a good length for a drill session. If you feel your mind wandering, walk off the court and return only when you're mentally ready to practice again.

Charlie Brumfield's first teacher demanded absolute concentration, admonishing students, "If you can't concentrate today, go do something else off the court and come back when you're ready."

Shannon Wright, holder of five women's national titles, says, "My attention span is crucial to the amount of time I practice. I drill only twice a week, a half hour per session. That's all I feel I need or care to concentrate on specific shots. The rest of the time I concentrate on playing racquetball against good players, jogging, and doing some weight training. But I don't do anything unless my heart is in it." Shannon's concentration and knowledge of her attention span has paid off for her.

Every drill in this book is organized in the following manner:

Objective: The particular physical and/or mental skill that you will develop through consistent repetition of the drill.

Steps: How to execute the drill. The steps involved will be explained and, where possible or profitable, illustrated.

Summary: This will prescribe the amount of time you need to spend on the drill, what common errors to watch out for when you practice, and what to concentrate on when doing the drill.

2

Warming Up

OBJECTIVE: Warming up before practicing or playing prepares the body for sudden and demanding maneuvers. Poor warming up is the culprit in more than half of all athletic injuries.

The warmed-up, well-stretched body can cover more court area. Flexibility helps you get your swings into the right groove.

Steps

Do a few knee bends. Touch your toes. After two or three minutes of this, do several jumps—ten is fine. Flex your shoulders, stretch your racquet behind your back and try to pull it apart from either end. Finish with good hard pushes at the wall or, if you're with someone you like, do the rowing exercise shown for twenty counts.

The point is, don't rush right onto the court and start swinging. Some of the pros do two or three laps around the court when they first go on court.

SUMMARY: A racquetball player should spend five to ten minutes doing warm-up exercises before the game.

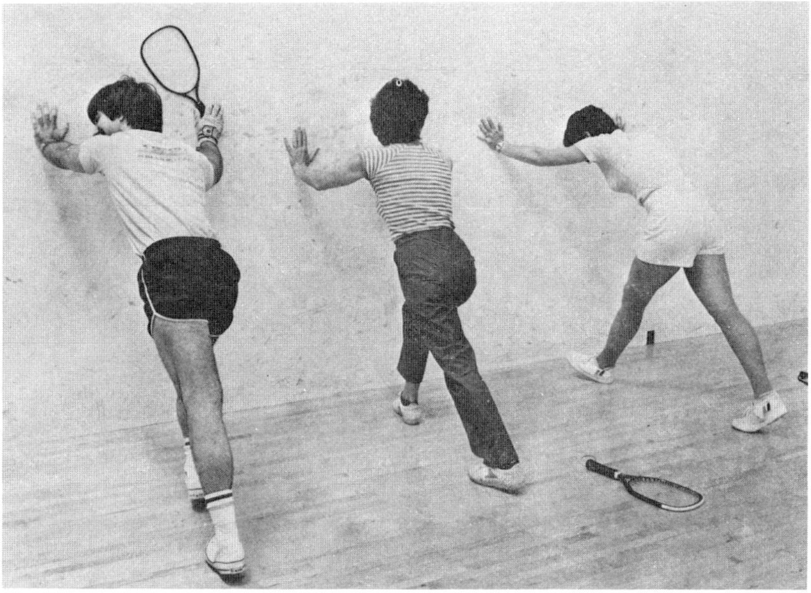

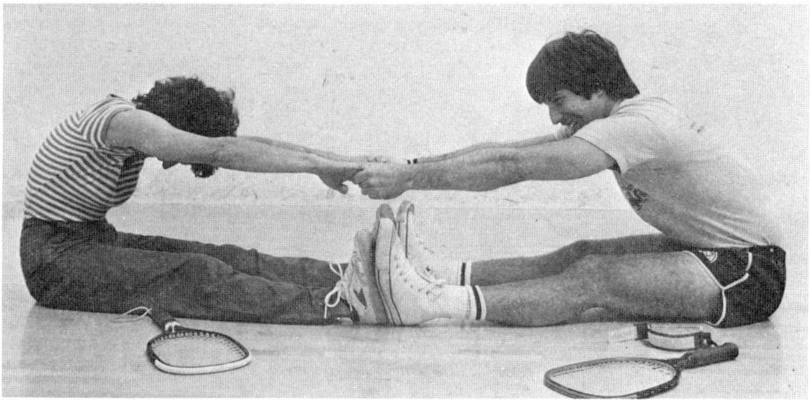

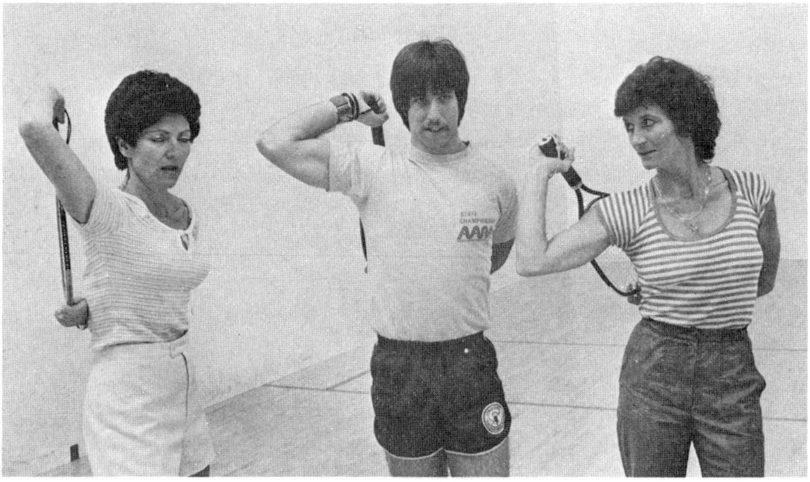

3
Drills for the Intermediate Player

A. OFF-THE-FRONT-WALL DRILL

OBJECTIVE: To develop the ability to kill or shoot the ball as it comes off the front wall. This is the most commonly missed shot in raquetball matches at all levels.

Steps

1. Stand in center court, facing the side of the court of the stroke on which you are working.
2. Using the off hand, toss the ball so that it hits the front wall first, ten feet above the floor, and bounces back, landing in front of you.
3. Shuffle forward and shoot a corner pinch (see diagram A), a straight kill (see diagram B and photo), a down-the-line shot (see diagram C), and a cross-court kill (see diagram D).

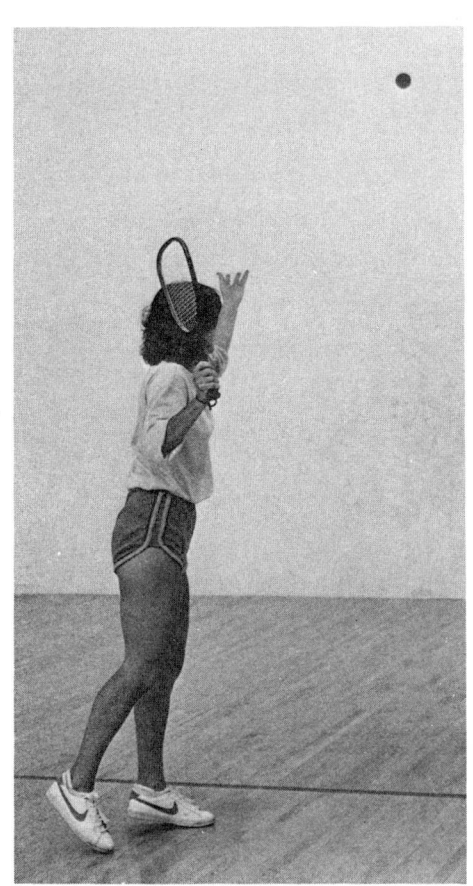

Step 2

Step 3

Diagram A

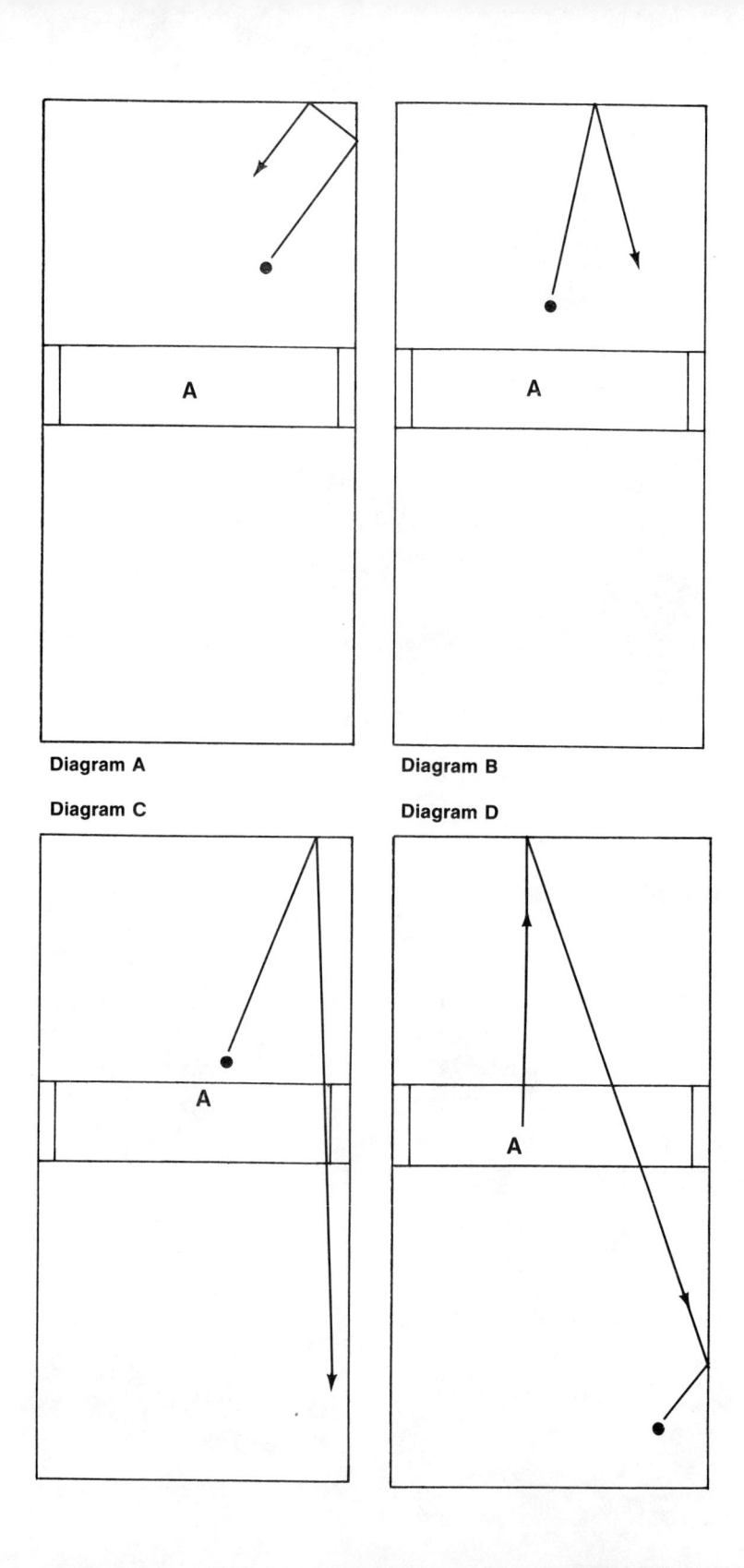

Diagram B

Diagram C

Diagram D

SUMMARY: Keep your eye on the ball. Make sure that your racquet is back high and early.

Do not practice cross-court passes. All you are doing with this difficult shot is leaving the ball up for your opponent to retrieve.

Repetition develops your front wall "killability." There is often more time to get your body into this shot than you would imagine. When you are in a slump, start working on your timing of shots up front.

B. STRAIGHT KILL DROP AND HIT DRILL FOR FOREHAND AND BACKHAND

OBJECTIVE: To enable you to hit a straight kill, beginning from the standing position, bending your body to meet the ball, and killing it straight down the line in front of you.

Steps

1. Position yourself just behind the short line a comfortable distance from the forehand side wall or backhand side wall.
2. With the off hand, toss the ball up and out in front of you so that you will have room to step over to the ball.

3. Do not begin your stroke until you hear the ball bounce. This automatically forces you to wait to hit the ball so that you do not hit it prematurely.

4. As the ball begins its final downward flight to the floor, you also lower your racquet and get your legs and lower body into the shot. Enlisting those legs and lower body is part of advancing your game.

12   Intermediate Racquetball Drills

5. Contact is made below knee level and the ball is driven into the front wall first with a snap of the wrist. To hit the ball straight in for the kill, hit the ball over slightly from where you are positioned, not behind yourself.

VARIATIONS: This drill can be practiced in front of the service area in front court and also from deep court.

SUMMARY: Keep your eye on the ball! Be sure to wait for the ball to bounce the first time before you begin your swing. This will help teach you the timing that is so important when killing a ball; that is, to wait until the ball has dropped to its lowest possible point before striking it. Of course, judgment becomes a factor, but timing is the most important component of this developing skill.

C. CORNER PINCH DROP AND HIT DRILL

OBJECTIVE: To learn to shoot the most precise kill shot in the game; to start to learn strategy. These shots are practiced with the opponent in mind.

Steps

1. Position yourself just behind the short line and a comfortable distance from the side wall. Imagine your opponent just behind you on the same side of the court. (See diagram.)

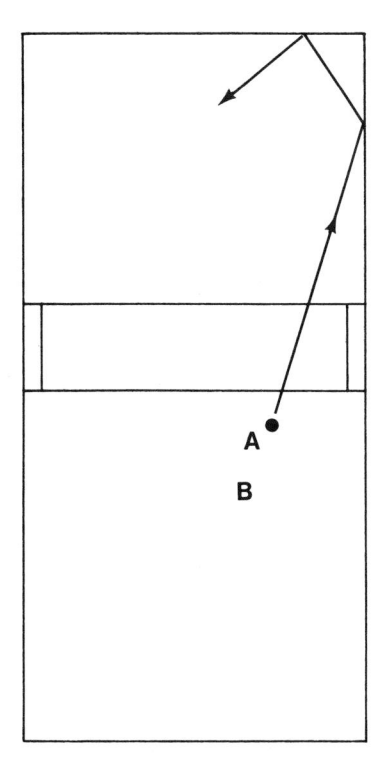

2. Toss the ball in front of you and out to the side.

3. Step into the shot and snap the ball to the side wall first, at knee level or below, no more than two feet out from the side wall.

VARIATIONS: This drill can be practiced from front court (in front of the service zone) and also from deep court.

SUMMARY: It may seem boring, but the drop and hit drill is your ticket to a near-pro performance. By varying the place where you drop the ball, you get a wide variety of practice shots. The corner pinch kill shot, a side wall-front wall drive that caroms off the wall hard and low is what you are trying to learn. It is one of the best tools in the arsenal of a good racquetball player.

D. SIDE WALL DRILL

OBJECTIVES: To advance your footwork; to teach you how to set up your body and shoot balls that are coming off the side wall. Most players do not set up properly for balls off the side wall and it costs them points. They tend to crowd the ball and shoot it from a higher position than necessary.

Steps

1. Stand even with the receiving mark, an arm-and-racquet's length from the side wall. Touch the racquet to the side wall so that you have established the fact that you are close enough to it.

Drills for the Intermediate Player 15

Step 1

16   Intermediate Racquetball Drills

2. Hold the ball in the fingertips of your off hand. Lightly and easily toss the ball high to touch the side wall.

3. As the ball comes down off the side wall, move away using a shuffling motion.

Drills for the Intermediate Player 17

4. Stop when you hear the ball bounce on the floor. Then begin your shuffle into the shot and hit the ball down the line for a pass (see diagram A), cross court for a pass (see diagram B), to the corner for a pinch kill (see diagram C), straight in for a kill (see diagram D).

Diagram A

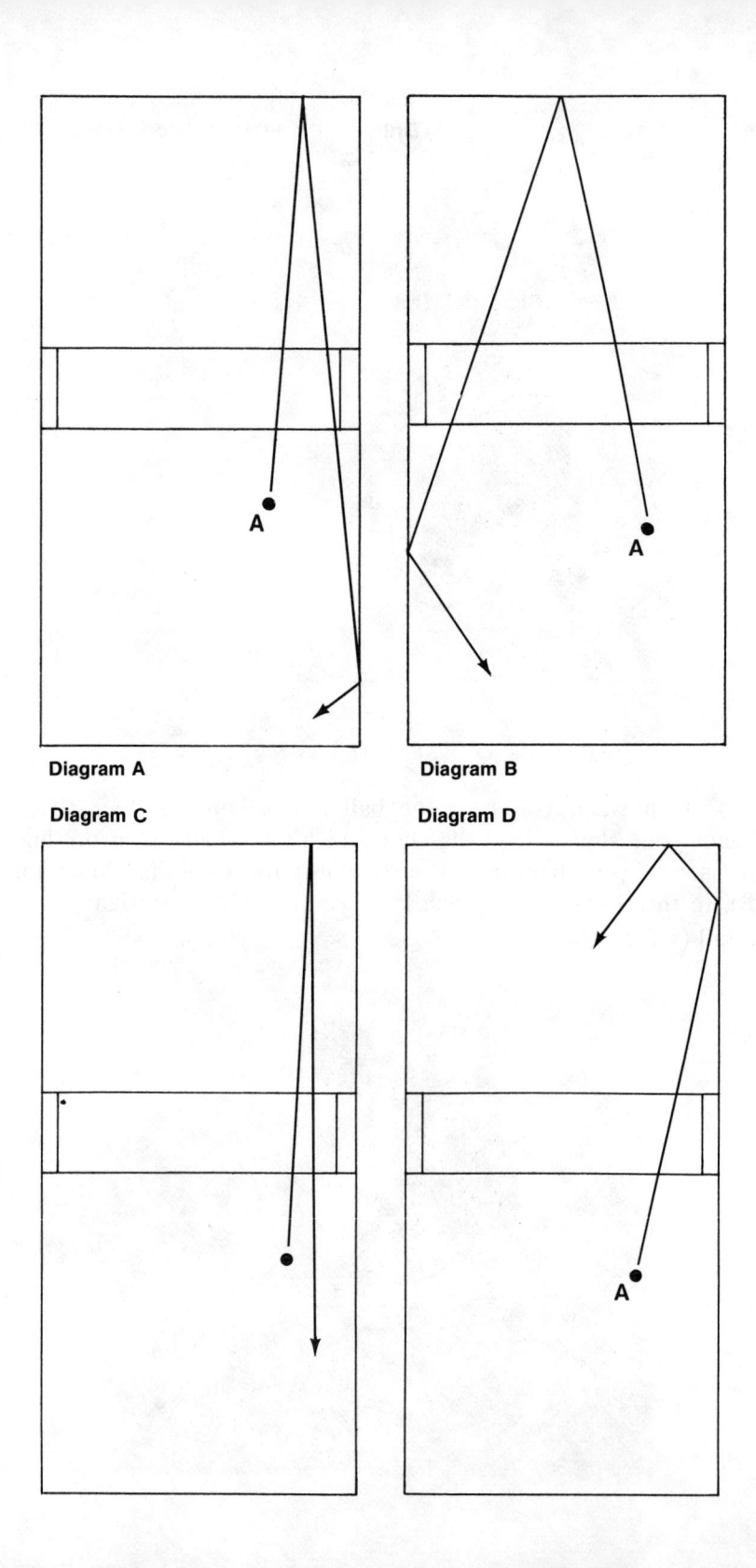

Diagram B

Diagram C

Diagram D

Drills for the Intermediate Player

5. Imagine your opponent in the correct spot for the shot you are practicing. Advanced play means *always* being aware of your opponent's position.

VARIATIONS: This drill can be done from front court and from deep court.

SUMMARY: Shuffle your feet at all times. Do not walk away; you will get caught off balance on the wrong foot. Use short steps and shuffle.

E. CORNER DRILL—BOUNCE IN

OBJECTIVE: To teach you to return the service skillfully. This is especially helpful for players who are having difficulty returning drive serves that are hit hard into the deep corners. It also helps you further develop your shooting ability.

Steps

1. In your mind, draw an imaginary four-foot-by-four-foot box in deep court. Stand a foot or two to the side of the box. Touch your racquet to the back wall for proper positioning in relation to the back wall. Pull your racquet up and back. The higher you pull your racquet up as you get set, the more power you will generate.

20   Intermediate Racquetball Drills

2. With the off hand, bounce the ball into the back wall first, one or two feet out from the side wall. The ball should then rebound around the deep corner of the court and pop slightly away from the side wall where you can get your racquet on it.

3. Step into the shot and successively hit the ball down the line for a down-the-line pass (see diagram A), straight in for a straight kill (see diagram B), to the ceiling for a ceiling shot (see diagram C), and to the corner for a corner pinch (see diagram D).

Drills for the Intermediate Player   21

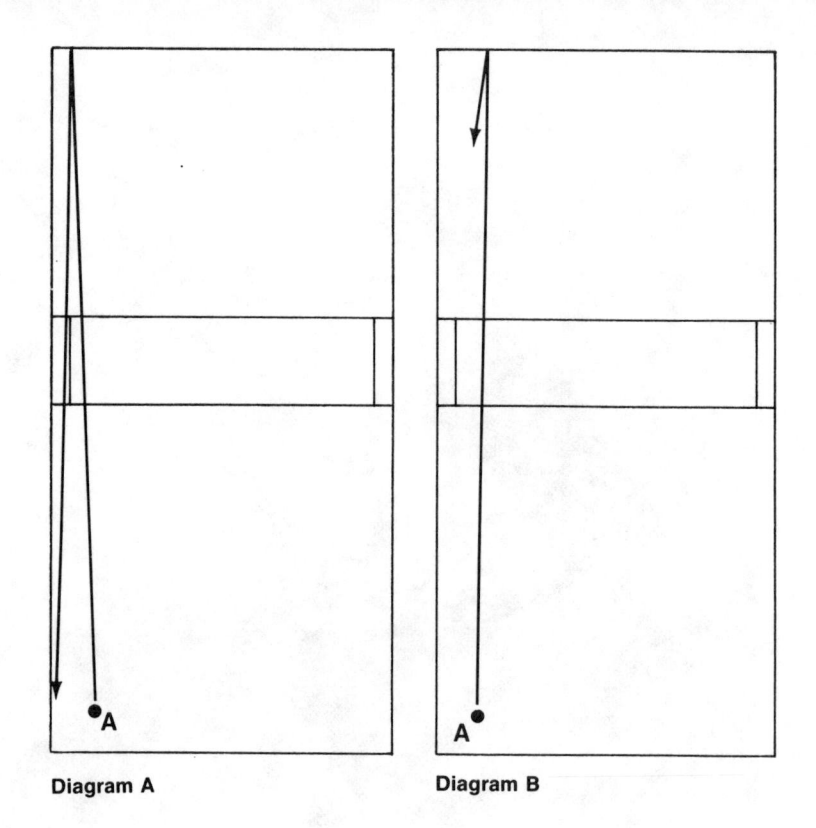

Diagram A

Diagram B

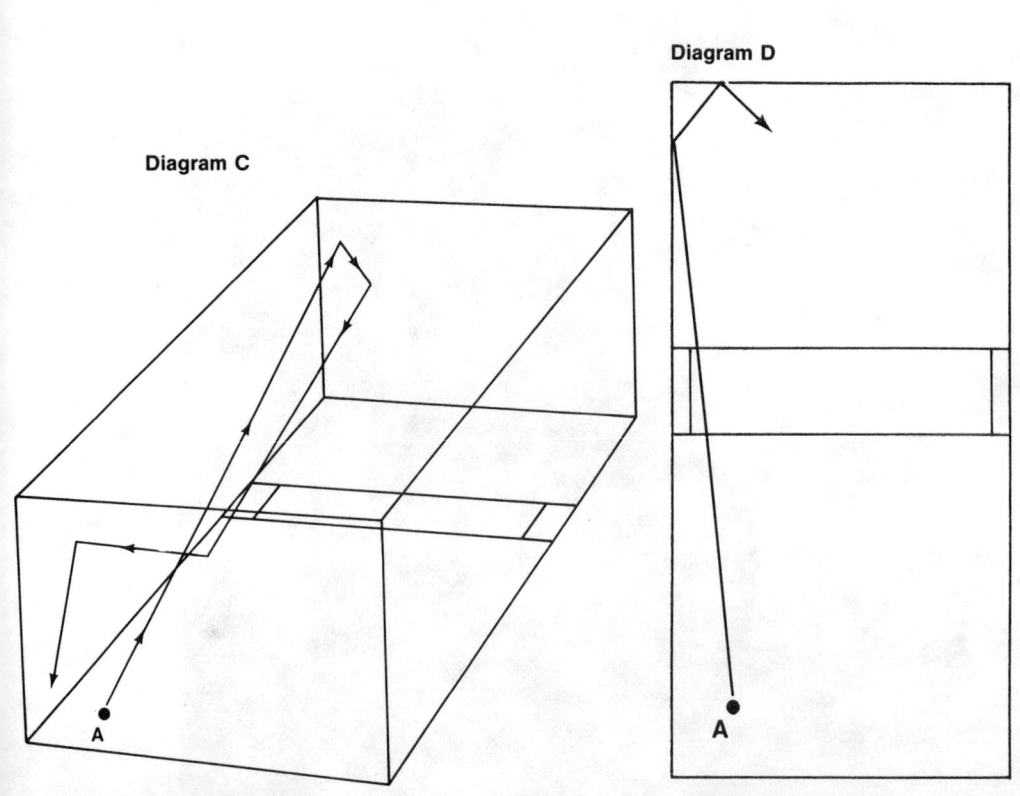

Diagram D

Diagram C

Drills for the Intermediate Player   23

SUMMARY: Keep your eye on the ball. Be sure to stay away from the ball so that you can step into the shot. Always start with the racquet back. Do not develop a two-swing motion toward the ball. A single smooth arc is desirable, not a chop.

F. CEILING BALL DRILL

OBJECTIVES: To increase your skill in ceiling-ball shot execution and to teach you to hit the ceiling ball down the line or cross-court. After a two-year absence the ceiling ball is now coming back as the young pros develop accuracy to go along with their speed.

Steps

1. Position yourself in the center of deep court. Position yourself an arm-and-racquet's length from the back wall.
2. To practice down the line, face your near side wall. Hit the ball to the ceiling first, slightly away from you so that the ball

24　Intermediate Racquetball Drills

rebounds down your near side wall, requiring another ceiling shot by your opponent (in this case, yourself). Keep the ball coming down the wall by constantly facing the side wall and hitting it down the line slightly away from the side wall so that all you can do to return it is hit it down the side wall again. Keep sliding that ball up and down the side wall until you can hit twenty-five balls where you want them without a mistake. Then try for one hundred! Pros often try the same shot in practice one hundred times in a row.

Drills for the Intermediate Player 25

26   Intermediate Racquetball Drills

3. To practice cross-court, start on the forehand side. Stand an arm-and-racquet's length from the side wall and from the back wall. Hit the ball cross-court by hitting it to the center of the ceiling. As the ball rebounds across the court to your backhand side, move cross-court, set up and return a backhand cross-court shot to your forehand side. Strive to keep the ball in play with these cross-court shots (see diagrams A and B).

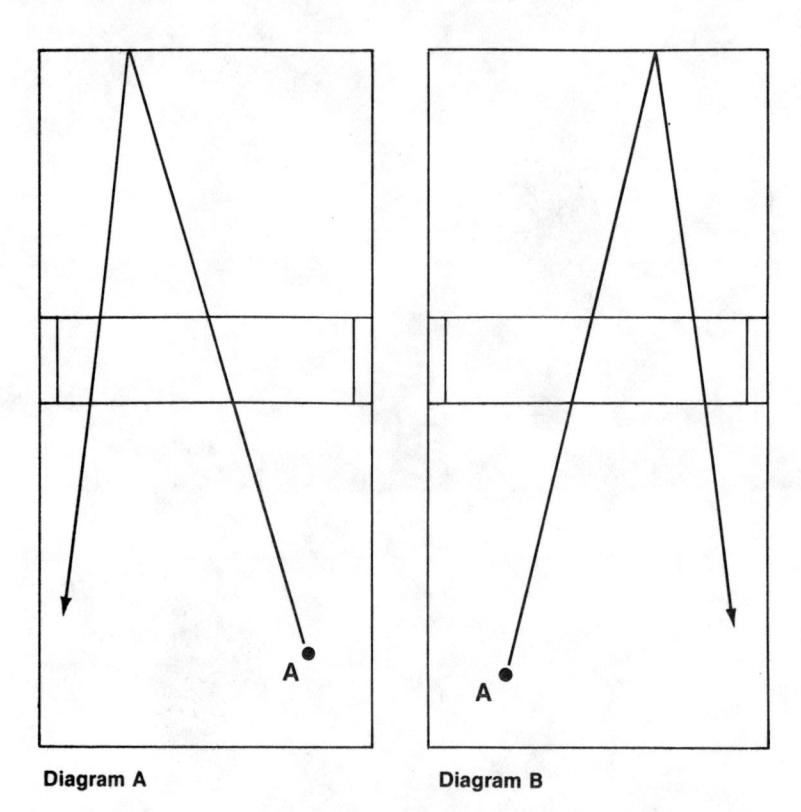

Diagram A   **Diagram B**

SUMMARY: Remember that ceiling balls in the intermediate level of play can be point makers if the angles down the line are so precisely hit that the ball dies in the back corners of the court. By constantly practicing these angles, you give your ceiling balls the best chance of forcing an opponent's error, a shot that you can put away, or, better yet, forcing a miss by your foe. Strive to hit your ceiling shots along these angles, and your point-making abilities will improve in direct proportion to your growing skill in placing the ball where you want it.

G. SHOOTING CEILING BALL OFF BACK WALL DRILL

OBJECTIVE: To teach you to recognize quickly when a ceiling is a setup off the back wall and not a defensive shot requiring another defensive shot. In short, an opportunity for an out or a point. Players who can wait for and shoot mishit ceiling balls coming as setups off the back wall are adding points to their game. They also cause panic in their opponents, who find their most precious defensive shot against lesser players turned against them by an improving intermediate player—you!

Steps

1. Get a live ball—the livelier the better, so that you can easily set yourself up with a ceiling ball off the back wall.
2. Stand an arm-and-racquet's length from the back wall. Hit the ball with good velocity to the ceiling and close to the front wall so that it rebounds high and off the back wall.

28   Intermediate Racquetball Drills

3. As the ball is coming, turn quickly and position yourself on the side with your racquet back early. Getting the racquet back early is the single most important factor when shooting off the back wall.

Drills for the Intermediate Player 29

4. Drop your legs slightly. Use plenty of wrist action when you contact the ball. Shoot the ball straight in for a kill or cross-court for a kill. Corner pinches are usually too hard to hit at first, but try some, anyway.

30   Intermediate Racquetball Drills

5. Practice the straight kill with your opponent's position in mind and practice the cross-court kill with your opponent in mind (see diagrams A and B).

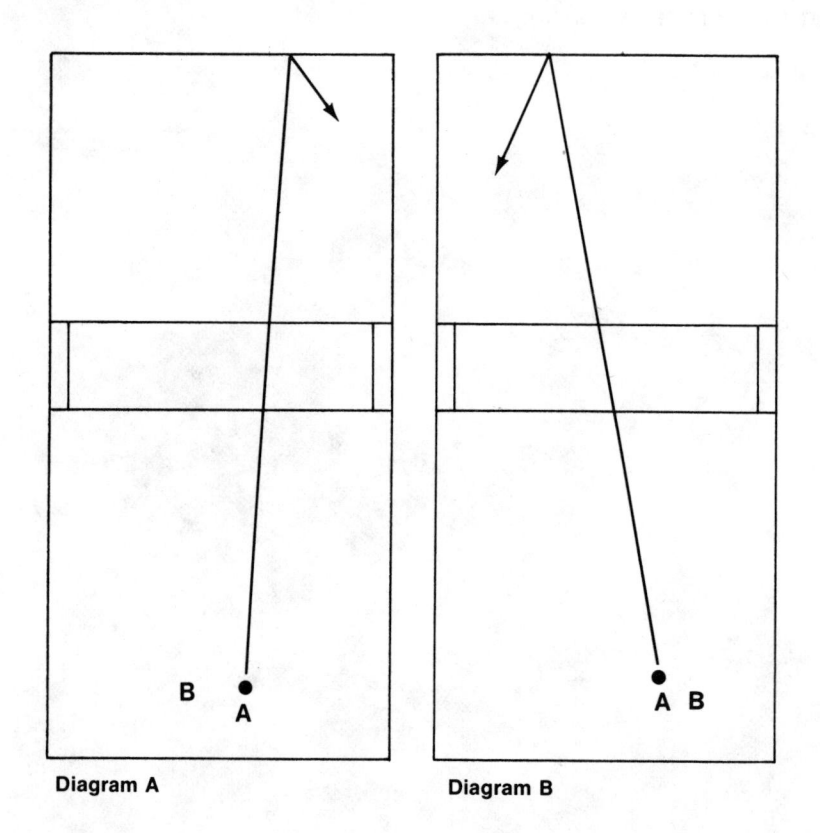

Diagram A

Diagram B

SUMMARY: Keep your eye on the ball and *do not pick your head up* until after you have contacted the ball. This shot requires the utmost concentration. So concentrate on the ball, not on where it's going. More points are lost in racquetball (and other ball sports) by taking your eye off the ball than by any other mental lapse.

4

Two-Player Drills

The two-player drills are designed so that players with varying degrees of expertise can work out productively with each other. The player with a deep-court problem can station him or herself in deep court and have the other player hit deep pinches, drives, or back wall shots. The player who tends to hang back in competition can practice returning front court lobs, thereby being forced to run toward the ball.

In these two-player drills, players can alternate between the "you" and "your opponent" positions. In the diagrams that follow, "A" indicates "you" and "B" indicates "your opponent."

A. RUNNING BACK FOR DEEP COURT SHOT DRILL

OBJECTIVE: To develop quickness and agility on court coverage, especially in the deep court when you are shooting. This drill prevents you from becoming lazy when moving to deep court. Instead of taking a higher shot than you normally would, you really run back, set yourself up, and shoot the ball. This drill will help rid you of the habit of cutting off a shot with a weak return.

32   Intermediate Racquetball Drills

Steps

1. Set up in the service zone, positioned exactly in center court and facing the side of the court where both you and your opponent are working. Your opponent positions himself behind you, facing the side of the court on which he will be shooting (see diagram A).

2. Hit a medium-speed ball just above waist height. The shot will die before the back wall in deep court. Your opponent immediately runs back once the ball has been hit and tries to get back far enough in time so that the ball drops in front of him. (see diagram B).

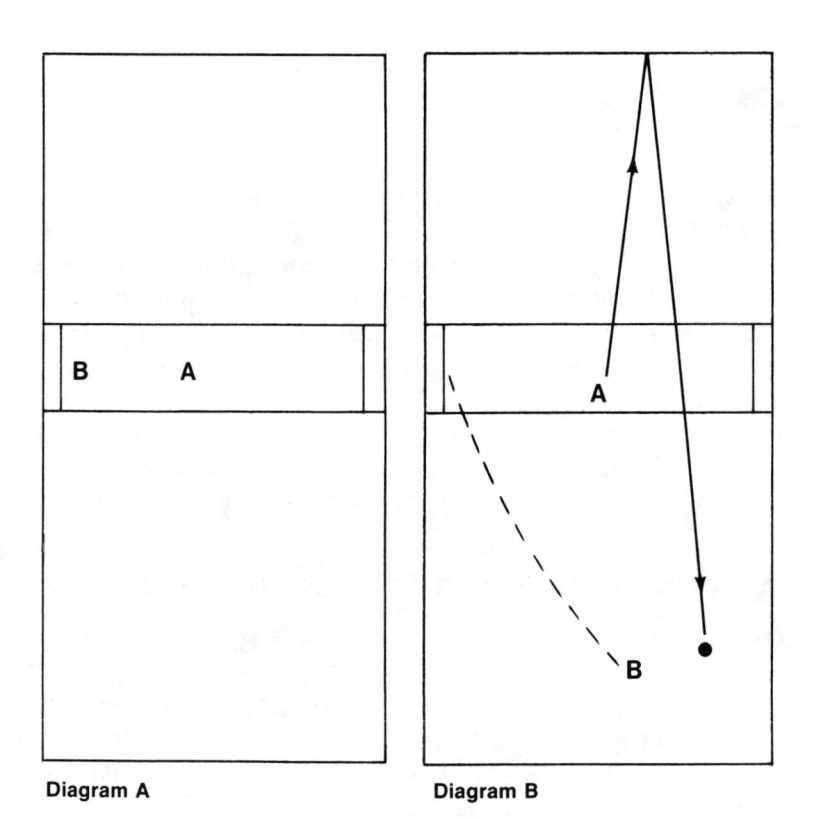

Diagram A

Diagram B

3. As the ball drops in front of him, your opponent steps forward and executes a down-the-line pass (see photo), a crosscourt pass (see diagram C), a straight kill (see diagram D), a corner pinch (see diagram E), and a ceiling ball if insufficient time to set up occurs.

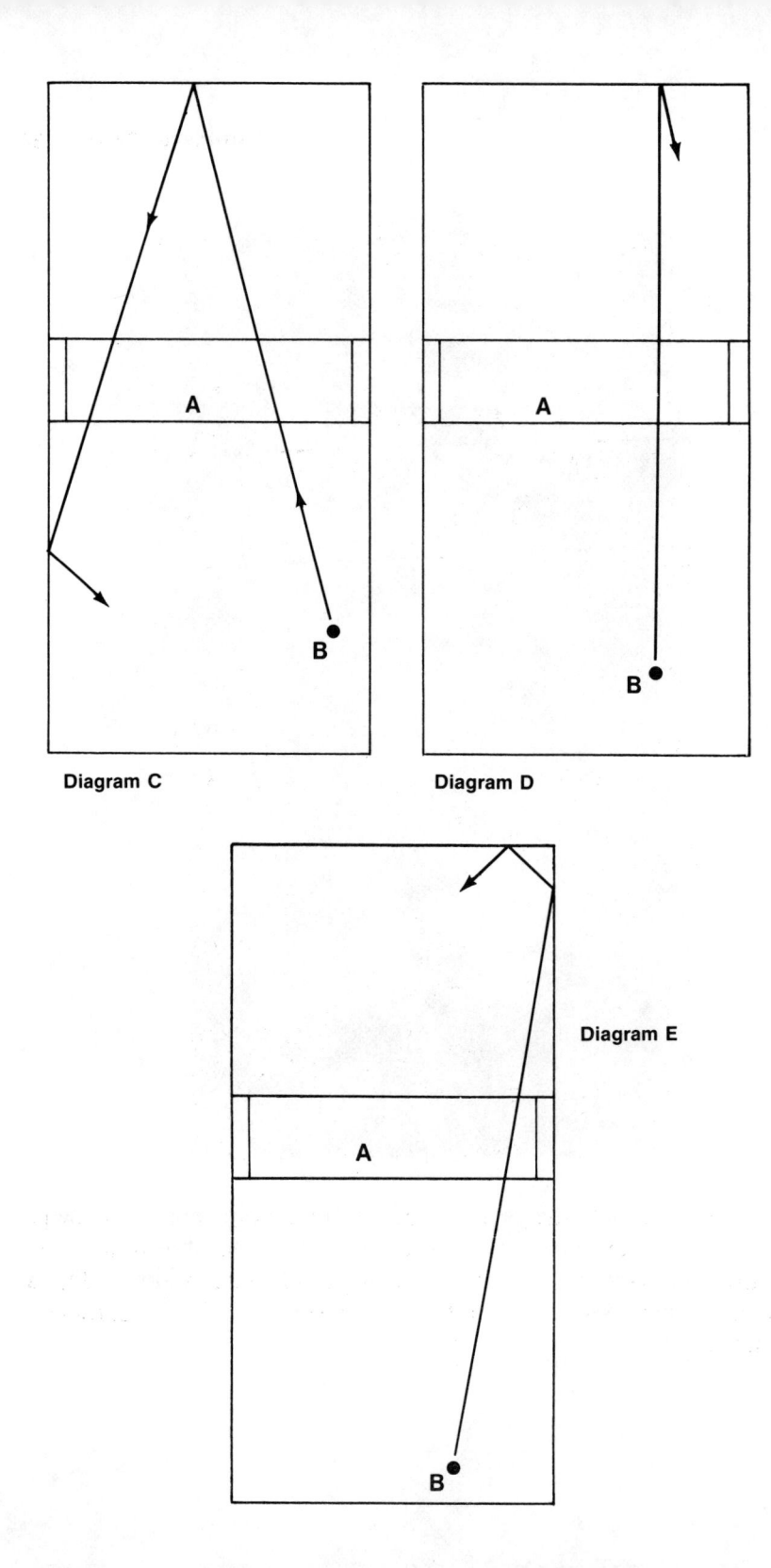

Diagram C

Diagram D

Diagram E

VARIATIONS: You and your opponent can make it harder for each other by varying the shots between those that come off the back wall and those that don't, forcing the shooter to determine instantly which is better—letting the ball come off the back wall and shooting it or taking it before it nears the back wall.

SUMMARY: The player setting up the opponent should remain in dead center. This allows the shooter to set up and shoot the right shot without fear of hitting the opponent. The player shooting the ball should shoot the shot that he needs to work on most and for which he has time to set up.

Each player sets up the other player ten times. The faster this exercise is done, the more aerobic the exercise is. Not only can you develop your skills; you can also get an especially good workout.

B. PINCH DRILL

OBJECTIVE: To develop reflexive ability—fast reactions—and to connect that ability to proper shot selection in terms of your opponent. Pinch shots, of course, hit side wall-front wall or front wall-side wall. The execution of this shot almost always separates the winning intermediate player from the loser.

Steps

1. Position yourself a step or two out of center court behind the short line at the receiving mark (see diagram A).

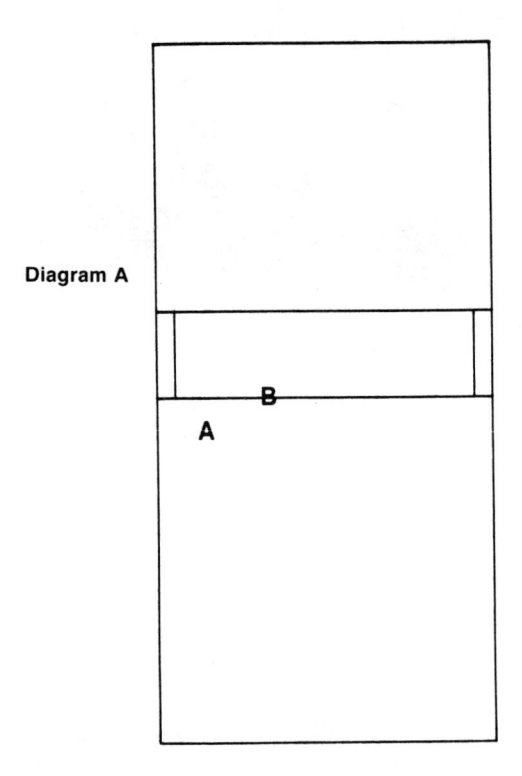

Diagram A

2. Your opponent positions himself on the short line or in center court (see diagram A).
3. Hit a down-the-line shot, medium speed at knee level (see photo).

38 Intermediate Racquetball Drills

4. Your opponent then steps across and pinches the ball for a side wall–front wall kill (see diagram B and photo), and kills the ball cross-court (see diagram C).

VARIATIONS: Players can play out the rally from this situation and keep score if they like.

Diagram B

Diagram C

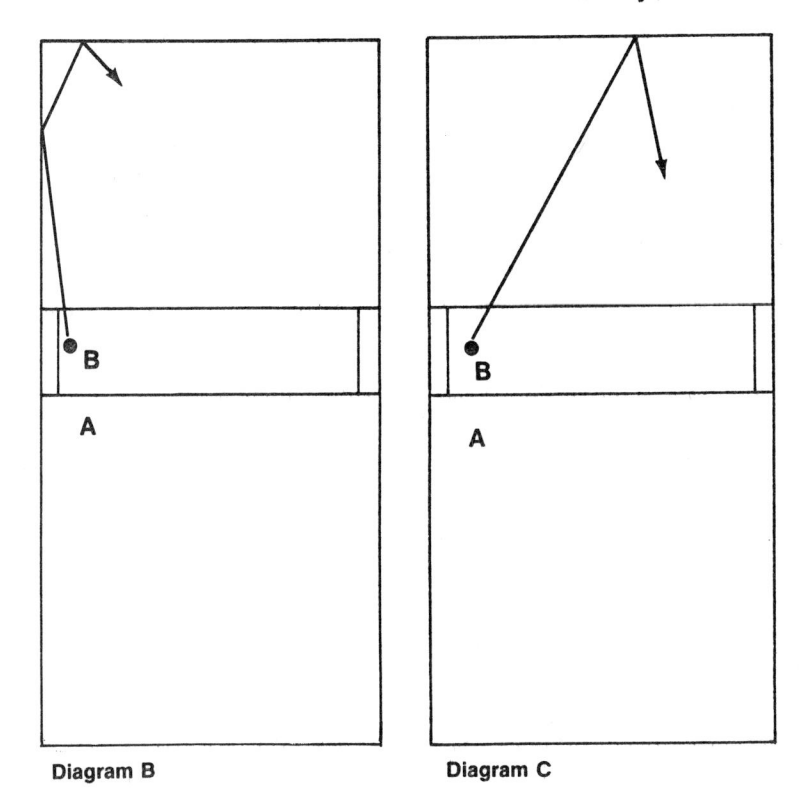

SUMMARY: Perfecting a good pinch shot is one of the shortcuts to raising your rating as a racquetball player. The sudden side wall–front wall carom of the ball throws your opponent off balance long enough for you to win the point. In practice with a partner you should alternate setting each other up for a succession of pinch shots—first to the forehand side of the hitter, then to the wall across from the hitter's body (the left wall for right-handers).

C. FLY-KILL DRILL

OBJECTIVE: With both players positioning themselves properly in the court, this drill develops skill in deciding when to fly-kill a ball as well as honing the ability to kill it. In the fly-kill, of course, you return the ball on the fly before it hits the floor. Surprise is a big factor in fly-shooting.

Steps

1. Position yourself facing the back wall at about the receiving mark, one step out of the center of the court. Your opponent positions himself on the short line, ready to move forward.
2. Hit the ball as a hard lob, designed to hit the back wall at chest level or above and carry all the way to the front wall so that when it rebounds on a fly off the front wall it takes its first bounce in front court. After you hit this setup shot, your opponent immediately sets up and prepares to scurry forward to kill the ball with a controlled sidearm stroke.

3. Your opponent kills the ball with a corner pinch if there is time to set it up, kills the ball straight in if there is not enough time for the corner pinch, and kills the ball cross-court if there is time to set up.

42   Intermediate Racquetball Drills

VARIATIONS: You and your opponent can play out the rally from this situation.

SUMMARY: The player shooting the ball must move forward. The least bit of hesitation will result in missing the ball or having to move back to take it on the bounce, giving your opponent time to get into center court position.

D. RUNNING TO FRONT COURT TO COVER A CORNER DRILL

OBJECTIVE: To develop quickness on the part of the player. Many players freeze in fear when they see a corner ball hit against them. This drill will quicken the retriever's reflexes. In short, the drill teaches you to cover the front court as well as deep court and midcourt and to replace that fear with hard-charging confidence.

Steps

1. See diagram one. Position yourself on the short line, one step closer to the side wall to which you are going to hit the ball (see diagram A).

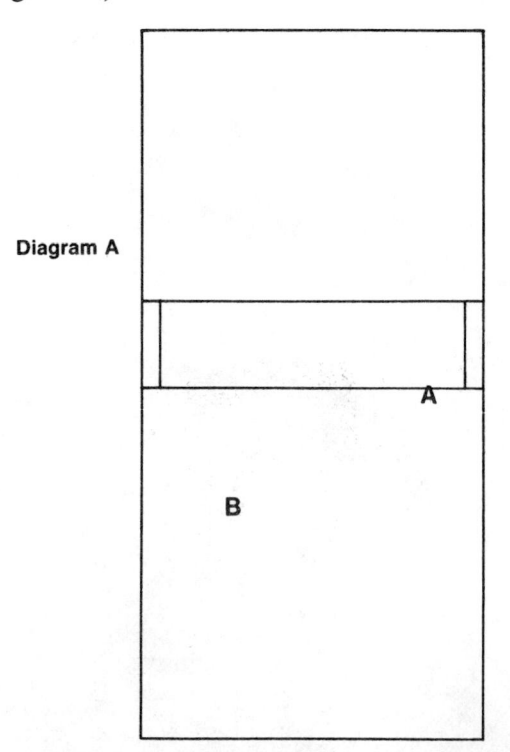

Diagram A

2. Your opponent positions himself behind you on the opposite side of the court (see diagram A).

3. Hit the ball to the side wall about two feet up and to the side of the front wall. The ball then rebounds to the opposite side of the front court, bouncing in such a way that it must be hit before it hits the opposite side wall.

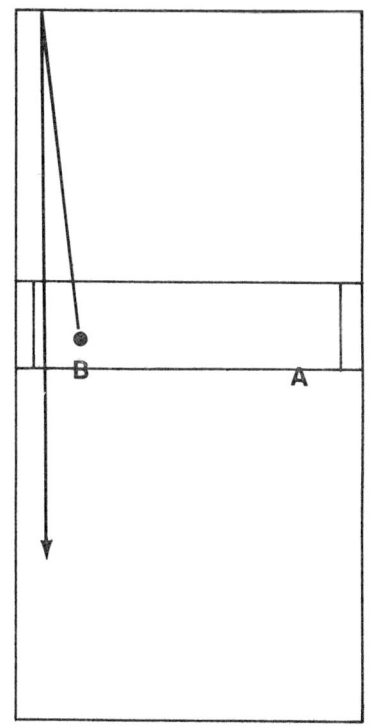

Diagram B

44   Intermediate Racquetball Drills

4. Once your opponent sees the shot hit, he runs up to retrieve the ball. When he arrives at the scene, he sets up and shoots the ball down the line, if he has time to set up (see diagram B), sets up and shoots the ball in for a straight kill (see diagram C), and hits the ball cross-court, catching the side wall just behind the opponent for a clean pass. This is done only if

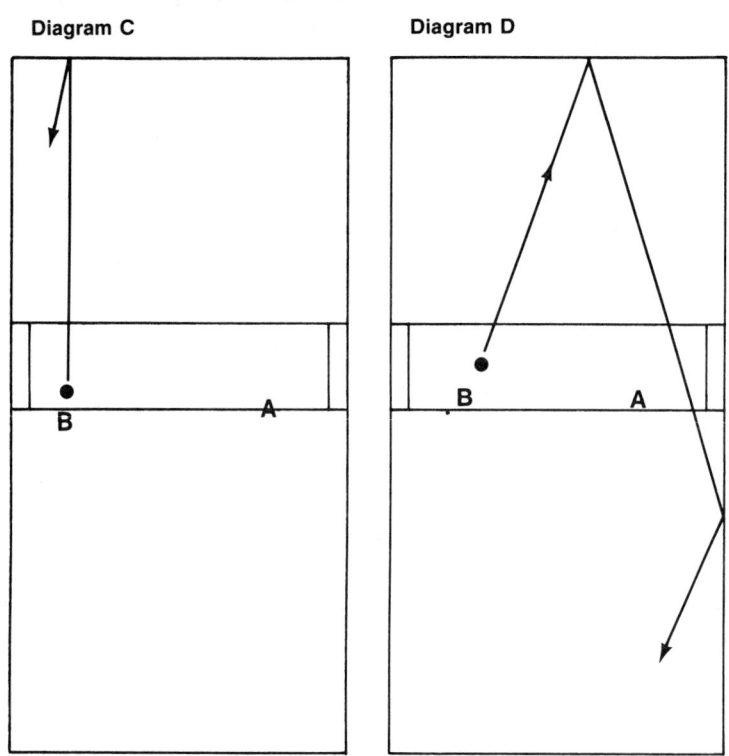

Diagram C

Diagram D

the player arrives to find that the ball is in front of him (see diagram D).

SUMMARY: Remember, the shot that is selected to hit is determined only by whether or not you have time to set up and shoot.

E. CEILING BALL AND SHOT DRILL

OBJECTIVE: To help players shoot ceiling balls. A ceiling ball rally between two good prayers could go on forever, theoretically. So what determines when and where to shoot the ball? This drill is designed to improve your ceiling game and your shot selection when bringing the play down from the ceiling to the floor.

Steps

1. You and your opponent begin hitting ceilings to each other. Each is trying to hit the perfect ceiling ball, that is, one that

46 Intermediate Racquetball Drills

lands in the back three feet of the court, over the head, requiring another ceiling return.

2. Eventually, of course, one of the players will miss. If the player competely misses the ball, the player whose turn it is to hit it picks it up and starts the rally again. This happens only in the case of the dead ball.

3. If one of the players hits the ball long, it rebounds off the back wall. The other player sets up and shoots it straight in for a kill (see diagram A), cross-court for a kill (see diagram B), down the line for a pass (see diagram C), or cross-court for a pass (see diagram D).

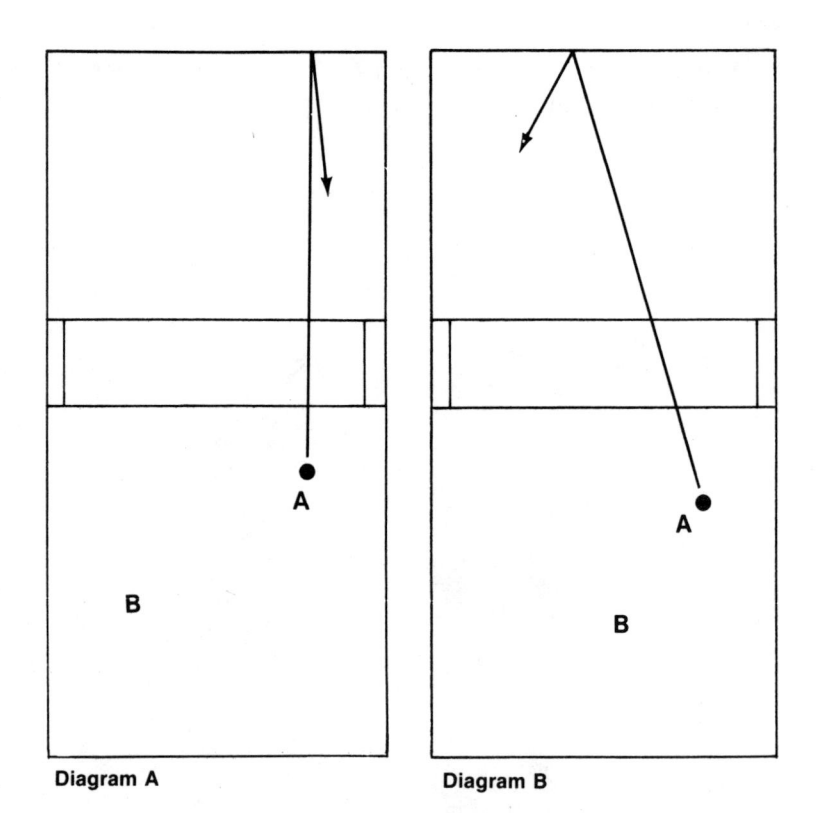

Diagram A

Diagram B

Two-Player Drills 47

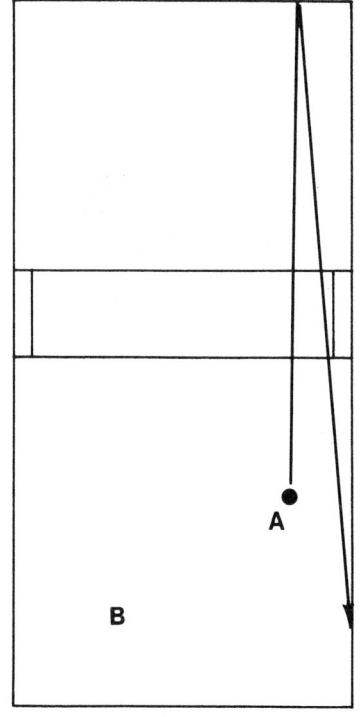

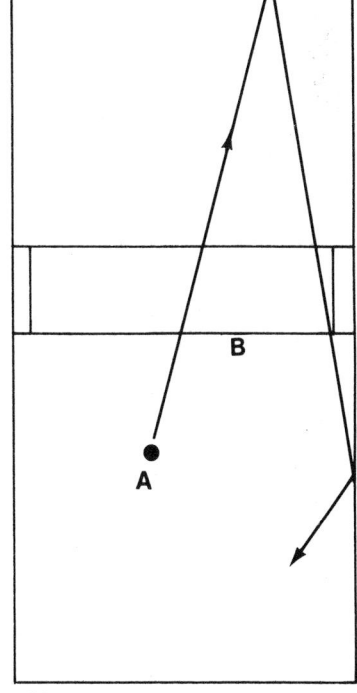

Diagram C

Diagram D

48   Intermediate Racquetball Drills

4. If one player does not hit the ball hard enough and it falls in front court for a setup, the other player sets up and shoots a near-corner pinch (see diagram E) or a near-side straight kill (see diagram F).

5. That player takes the shot, then you simply begin the rally again, resuming the number count from where you left off.

Diagram E **Diagram F**

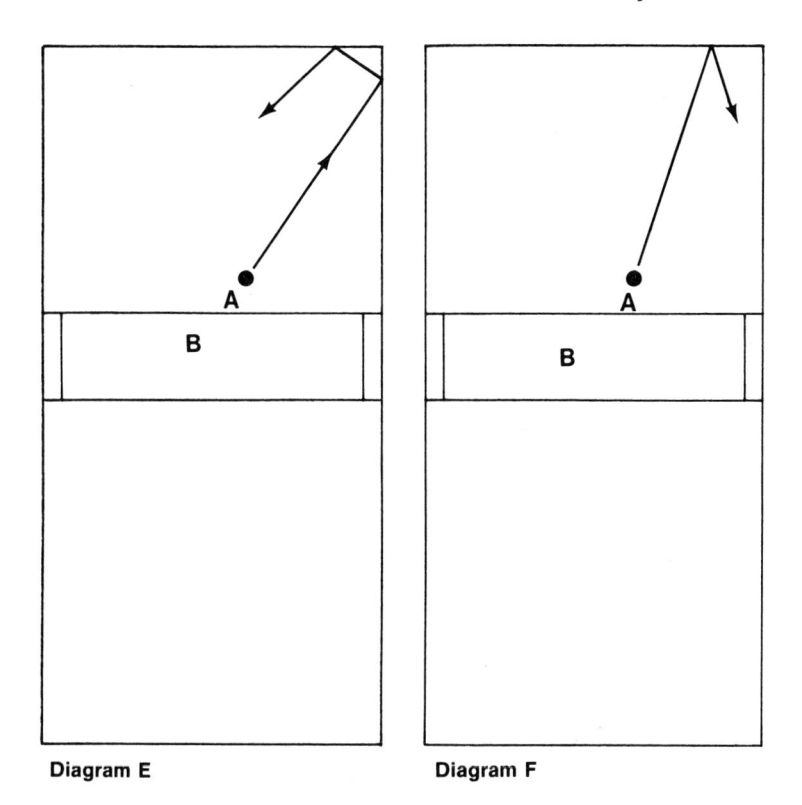

SUMMARY: Practice hitting one hundred balls on the forehand side only, then fifty balls on the backhand side, then one hundred balls on alternating sides.

F. DRIVE SERVE AND SERVICE RETURN DRILL

OBJECTIVE: To make you stronger server and better strategic service returner.

Steps

1. Position yourself in the service zone for a drive serve.
2. Your opponent positions himself in deep court for the return. He positions himself farther forward than the beginner, an arm and a half's racquet length from the back wall.

3. Drive the serve to your opponent.
4. Your opponent must base his shot on two factors: where you are and which wall he is going to play the ball off.
5. Possible serve returns include the following:
   (a) Ball off the side wall: down the line if your opponent remains in the center (see diagram A); pinch if your opponent crowds you (see diagram B); ceiling, if your opponent is quick and covers your returns well.

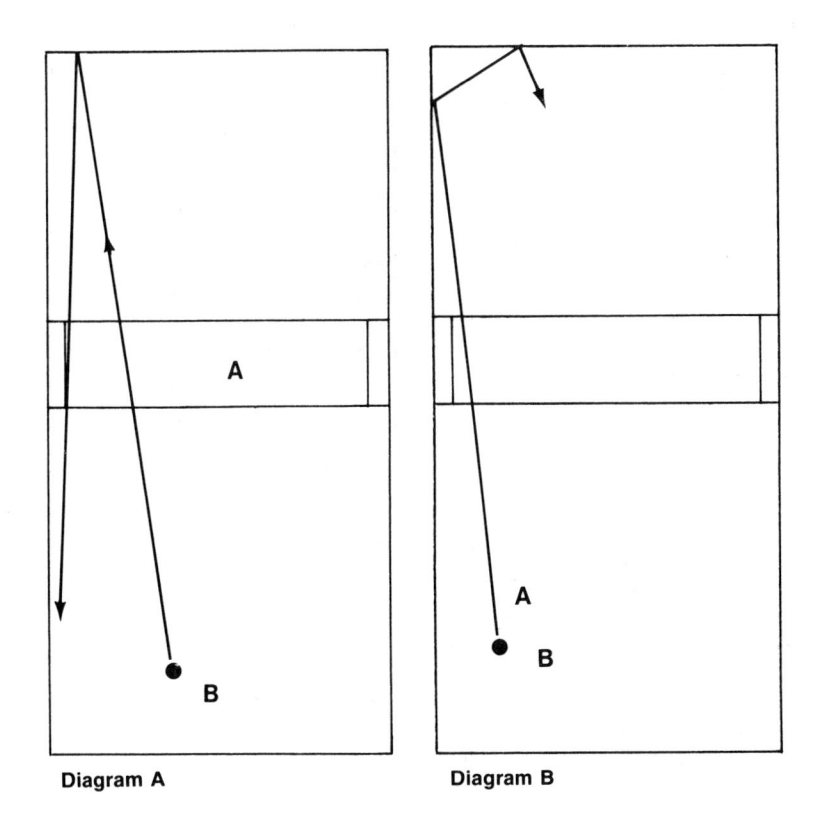

Diagram A   **Diagram B**

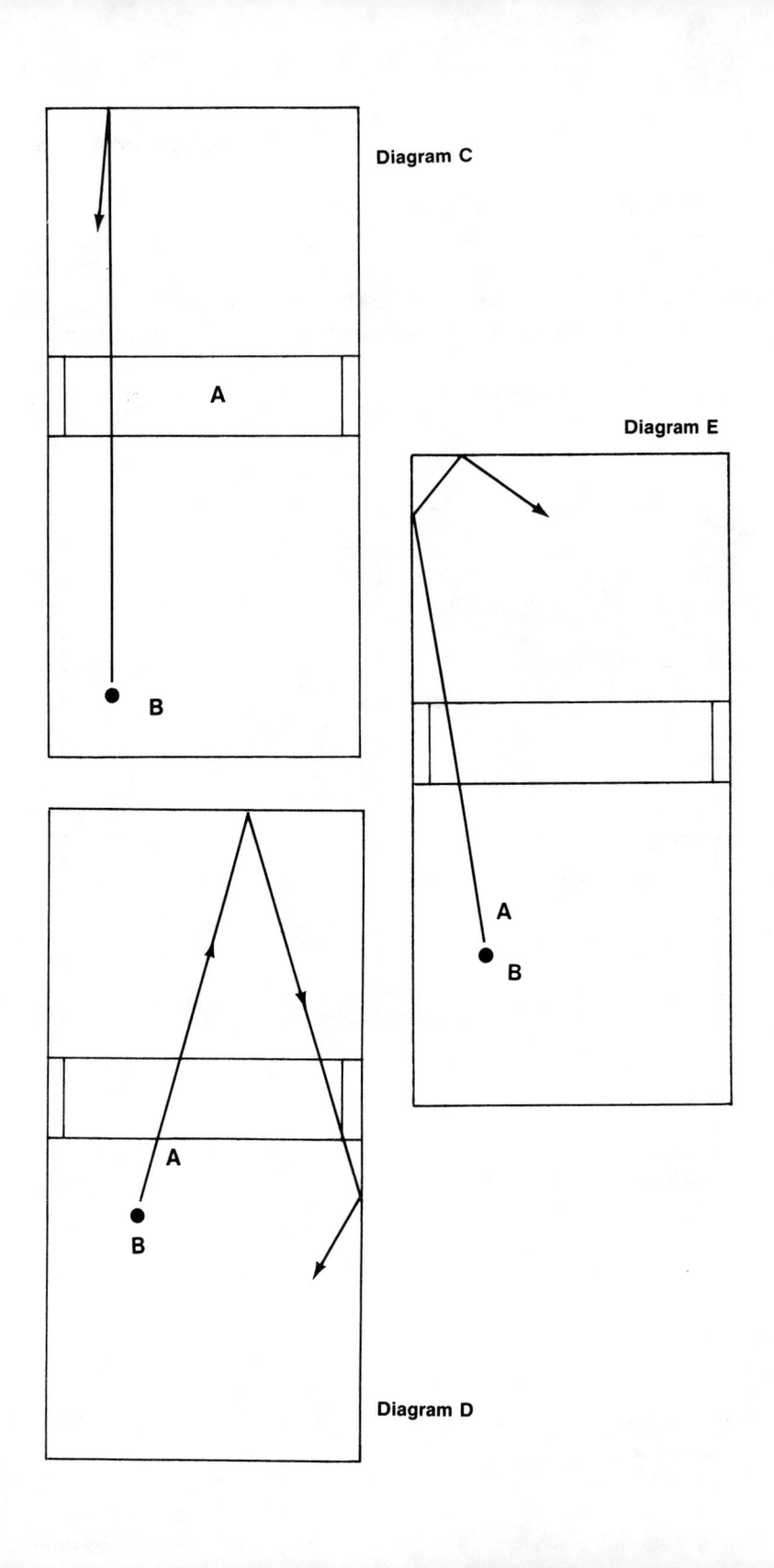

Diagram C

Diagram E

Diagram D

(b) Ball off the back wall: straight kill if your opponent remains in the center (see diagram C); cross-court pass if your opponent comes to your side of the court or remains in center (see diagram D); pinch if your opponent is on your side of the court (see diagram E); go to the ceiling shot only if the ball pops out in such a way that your return shot will result in a setup or a skip.

6. Then both players play out the rally.
7. The player who wins the rally serves; the player who loses the rally receives.

SUMMARY: Really concentrate on from which wall you are playing the ball. Also, vary your shots a lot. The more unpredictable your service returns, the more formidable your game.

As the server, try to angle the ball into the corner (see photo). Ideally, you want an ace or a setup return every time you strike the ball.